Atheneum Books for Young Readers

New York   London   Toronto   Sydney   New Delhi

P-E-C-T

Aretha Franklin, The Queen of Soul

Carole Boston Weatherford

illustrated by **Frank Morrison**

ATHENEUM BOOKS FOR YOUNG READERS

An imprint of Simon & Schuster Children's Publishing Division

1230 Avenue of the Americas, New York, New York 10020

ATHENEUM BOOKS FOR YOUNG READERS is a registered trademark of Simon & Schuster, Inc. Atheneum logo is a trademark of Simon & Schuster, Inc. For information about special discounts for bulk purchases, please contact Simon & Schuster Special Sales at 1-866-506-1949 or business@simonandschuster.com.

The Simon & Schuster Speakers Bureau can bring authors to your live event. For more information or to book an event, contact the Simon & Schuster Speakers Bureau at 1-866-248-3049 or visit our website at www.simonspeakers.com.

Book design by Debra Sfetsios-Conover

The text for this book was set in Superclarendon.

The illustrations for this book were rendered in oil paint.

Manufactured in China

0421 SCP

10 9 8 7 6 5

Library of Congress Cataloging-in-Publication Data

Names: Weatherford, Carole Boston, 1956- author. | Morrison, Frank, 1971- illustrator.

Title: Respect : Aretha Franklin, the queen of soul / Carole Boston Weatherford ; illustrated by Frank Morrison.

Description: [First edition.] | New York City : Atheneum Books for Young Readers, 2020. | Includes bibliographical references. | Audience: Ages 4 - 8 | Audience: Grades K-1 | Summary: "Aretha Franklin was born to sing. The daughter of a pastor and a gospel singer, her musical talent was clear from her earliest days in her father's Detroit church. Aretha sang with a soaring voice that spanned more than three octaves. Her incredible talent and string of hit songs earned her the title "the Queen of Soul." This Queen was a multi-Grammy winner and the first female inductee to the Rock and Roll Hall of Fame. And there was even more to Aretha than being a singer, songwriter, and pianist: she was an activist, too. Her song "Respect" was an anthem for people fighting for civil rights and women's rights. With words that sing and art that shines, this vibrant portrait of Aretha Franklin pays her the R-E-S-P-E-C-T this Queen of Soul deserves"— Provided by publisher.

Identifiers: LCCN 2019035643 | ISBN 9781534452282 (hardcover) | ISBN 9781534452299 (eBook other)

Subjects: LCSH: Franklin, Aretha—Juvenile literature. | Soul musicians—United States—Biography. | African American singers—Biography—Juvenile literature. | Singers—United States—Biography—Juvenile literature.

Classification: LCC ML3930.F68 W43 2020 | DDC 782.421644092 [B]—dc23

LC record available at https://lccn.loc.gov/2019035643

To Cara and Jordin: Always have a song in your soul.

—C. B. W.

To my two extraordinary divas, Nia and Tiffani:

Be good, be great.

—F. M.

B-L-E-S-S-E-D

Cradled by the church, rocked by an ebony sea,
Aretha says a little prayer each night on bended knee.

D-E-T-R-O-I-T

The Franklins move north from Memphis, Tennessee.
They put down roots and rise like a mighty tree.

M-U-S-I-C

Hand-clapping gospel—the Franklins' pedigree.
Parents, children praise the Lord in stirring harmony.

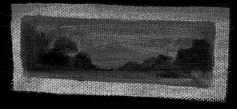

S-T-R-I-F-E

Clarence and Barbara Franklin can't seem to agree.
Daddy wasn't faithful, so Mama chose to flee.

G-I-F-T-E-D

Young, gifted, black, Aretha hears a melody.
Then she plays the tune by ear—plinking perfectly.

E-X-A-M-P-L-E

Her preacher father fights for rights in his community.
Other leaders visit to voice a common plea.

T-A-L-E-N-T

Young Aretha's solos soar with artistry.
Her wise father senses his daughter's destiny.

D-E-B-U-T

Fourteen, recording live, and nervous as can be.
She cuts a gospel album, gives God the victory.

V-O-I-C-E

Aretha's voice resounds with color and clarity,
spanning three-plus octaves, the maestros all agree.

R-I-G-H-T

For the civil rights movement for racial equality,
Aretha raises funds and gives concerts for free.

G-R-E-A-T

Aretha's crowned as Queen of Soul, our own royalty.
She wins awards and accolades, and more than one degree.

AUTHOR'S NOTE

Aretha Franklin (1942–2018) was a singer, songwriter, pianist, and civil rights activist. Hailed as the Queen of Soul, she was born into a religious and musical family in Memphis, Tennessee. In 1944 the Franklins moved to Detroit, Michigan. There, her father Clarence—a gospel singer known as the man with the "million-dollar voice"—became the pastor of New Bethel Baptist Church. Her parents separated when Aretha was six, and her mother Barbara—also a gospel singer—died four years later.

As a girl, Aretha learned to play piano by ear and sang with her sisters in the church choir. Touring the gospel music circuit with her father, she met singers Clara Ward and Mahalia Jackson and civil rights leader Martin Luther King Jr.

At age fourteen, Aretha recorded her first album, *Spirituals*. The music industry took notice, and by age eighteen, Franklin had landed a contract with Columbia Records. She later signed with Atlantic Records, where she recorded a parade of rhythm-and-blues (R&B) hits, including the song "Respect." In 1980, she joined Arista Records, where her sales figures continued to earn her gold records. With 88 hit singles, Franklin is one of the bestselling music artists in history. She was also one of the first African American artists to cross over and achieve success on both the R&B and pop charts.

Franklin was not just an artist, though; she was also an activist. During the 1960s, she performed at benefit concerts to support the civil rights movement and quietly donated funds to bail protesters out of jail.

Franklin appeared on television variety shows, and her music has been featured on soundtracks for many television shows and movies. She also acted in two films: *The Blues Brothers* (1980) and *Blues Brothers 2000* (1998).

Franklin had a powerful mezzo-soprano voice and a three-octave vocal range. During one awards show, she stood in for ailing opera star Luciano Pavarotti, astonishing everyone by singing the challenging aria "Nessun Dorma." When she was in her sixties, Franklin studied classical piano with a teacher who had trained at New York's Juilliard School of Music.

In her spare time, the mother of four enjoyed cooking. Family and friends called her by her nickname, "Ree-Ree."

For many years, Franklin's fear of flying limited her touring. However, that diminished neither her fame nor her accolades. She sang during inauguration festivities for presidents Carter and Obama. And Franklin scored numerous firsts, including becoming the first female inductee into the Rock & Roll Hall of Fame. She was also inducted into the Gospel Music Hall of Fame. During her career, she received eighteen Grammy Awards, the National Medal of Arts, and the Presidential Medal of Freedom. For her lifetime achievements, Franklin was named a Grammy Living Legend. In 2010, *Rolling Stone* magazine named her as the greatest singer of all time. In Detroit—Franklin's adopted hometown—an amphitheater is named in her honor.

CHART-TOPPERS: ARETHA FRANKLIN'S BIGGEST HITS

Respect

Baby I Love You

I Never Loved a Man (The Way I Love You)

Chain of Fools

(Sweet Sweet Baby) Since You've Been Gone

Think

Share Your Love With Me

Don't Play That Song (with The Dixie Flyers)

Call Me

Bridge Over Troubled Water

Spanish Harlem

Day Dreaming

Angel

I'm In Love

Until You Come Back to Me (That's What I'm Gonna Do)

Something He Can Feel

Break It to Me Gently

Jump to It

Get It Right

Freeway of Love

I Knew You Were Waiting (For Me) with George Michael